Let's Learn About Farm Machines

TRACTORS

Therese M. Shea

Enslow Publishing
101 W. 23rd Street
Suite 240
New York, NY 10011
USA
enslow.com

Words to Know

battery A tool that is used to operate machines using electricity.

crop A plant that is grown for food.

engine A machine that uses energy to operate something, like a car.

equipment Tools needed for a special purpose.

fuel Matter that is burned to produce power.

grip To grab or hold tightly.

harvesting Having to do with gathering crops.

pollution Matter that makes land, water, or air dirty and not safe to use.

tread The lines on a tire.

CONTENTS

Farmers use tractors to pull many different things.

Tractor Power!

Tractors are not fast. But they are powerful! That's why you may see them pulling heavy equipment. These machines are very useful. They help with many jobs on the farm.

Tractor tires are large and made to work in dirt and mud.

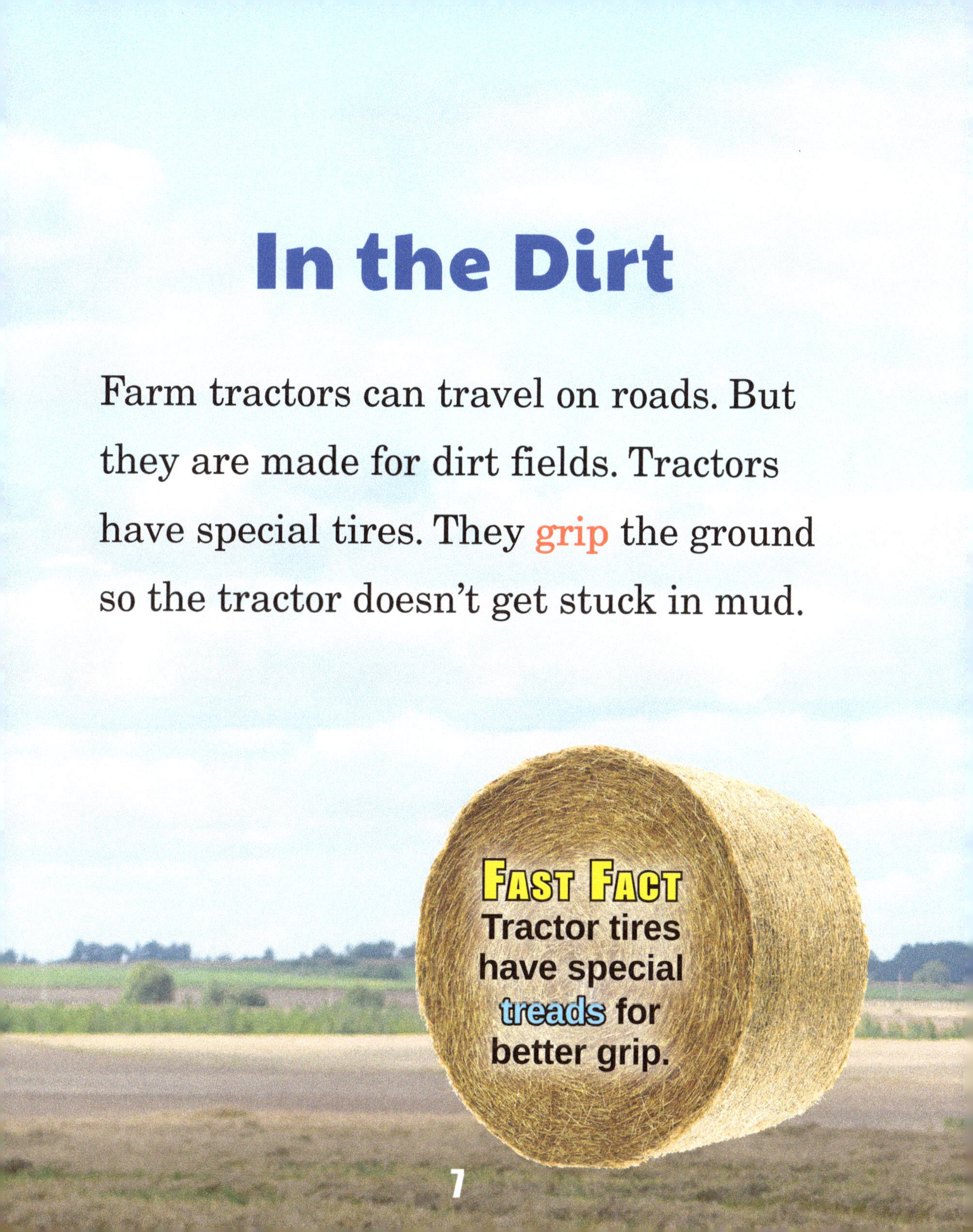

In the Dirt

Farm tractors can travel on roads. But they are made for dirt fields. Tractors have special tires. They grip the ground so the tractor doesn't get stuck in mud.

FAST FACT

Tractor tires have special treads for better grip.

Before tractors, horses pulled plows

Replacing Animals

Farmers did not always have tractors. They used horses and other strong animals to pull heavy equipment through fields. This took a lot of time and money. Tractors took the place of animals.

FAST FACT
It could take more than a dozen horses to pull some farm equipment!

Some tractors have a cover for drivers. Other tractors are open.

Open or Cab?

On some tractors, the driver sits in a seat open to the air. Others have an area with a covered seat. It is called a cab. The cab protects the driver from sun, rain, and cold.

Field workers load up a trailer with watermelons.

What They Pull

Tractors pull important farm equipment. They pull machines that plant seeds in the fields. They pull heavy harvesting equipment, too. They also pull trailers full of crops.

FAST FACT

Tractors pull people on hayrides, too!

A tractor pulls a spraying machine. The tractor's power takeoff allows the machine to run.

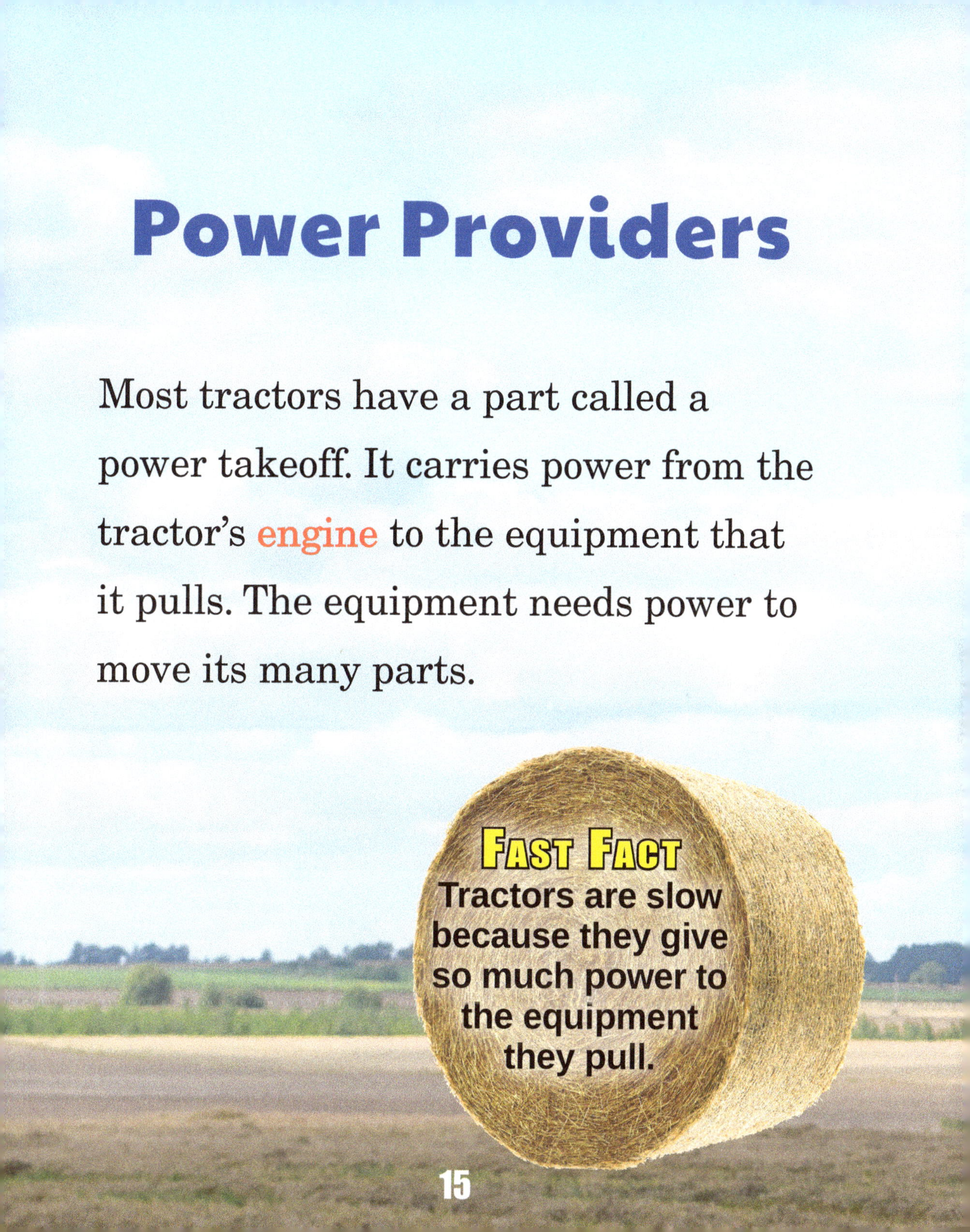

Power Providers

Most tractors have a part called a power takeoff. It carries power from the tractor's engine to the equipment that it pulls. The equipment needs power to move its many parts.

FAST FACT

Tractors are slow because they give so much power to the equipment they pull.

A farmer fills his tractor with gas.

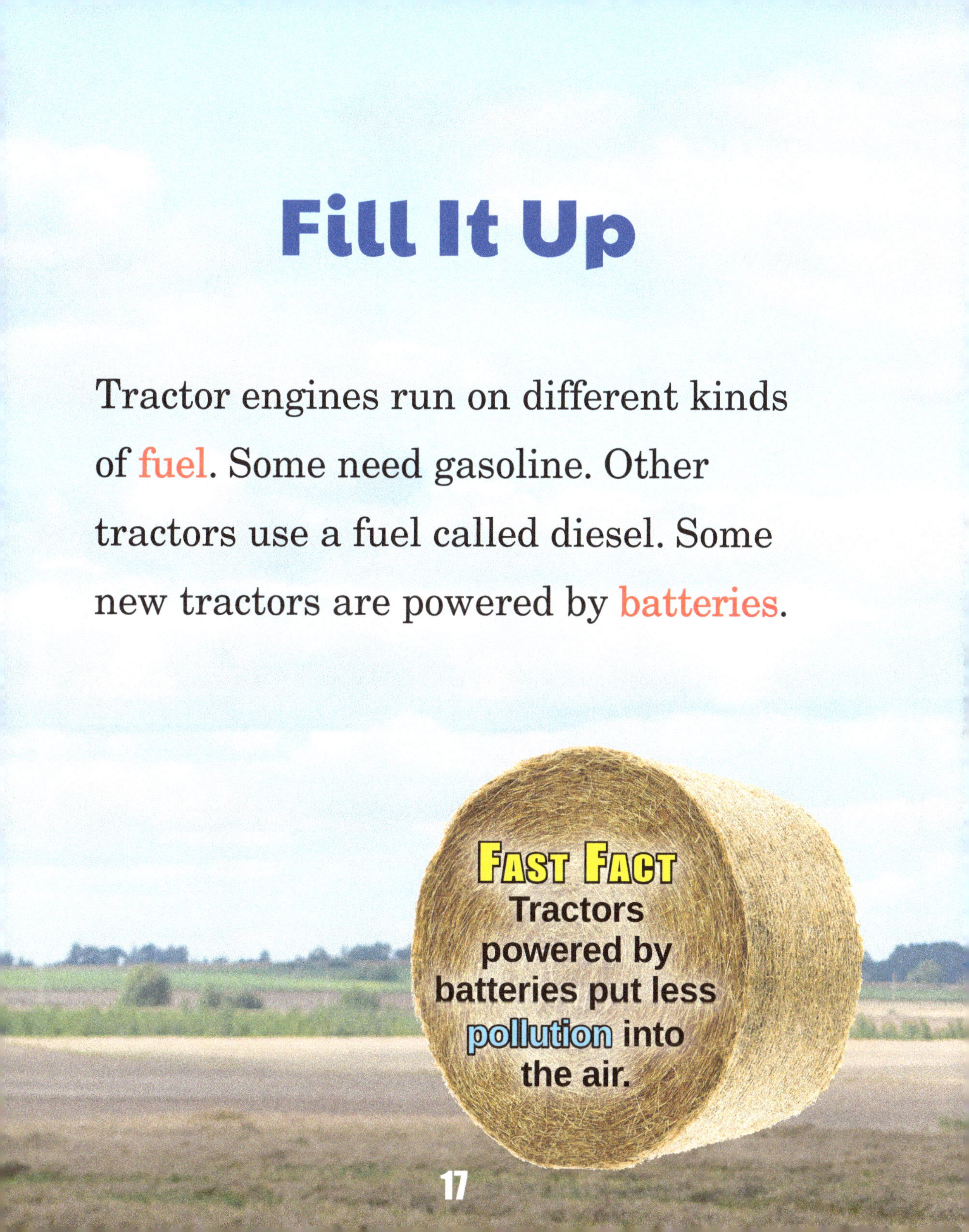

Fill It Up

Tractor engines run on different kinds of fuel. Some need gasoline. Other tractors use a fuel called diesel. Some new tractors are powered by batteries.

FAST FACT

Tractors powered by batteries put less pollution into the air.

This tractor is made by Lamborghini, the same company that makes expensive sports cars.

Modern Tractors

Today's tractors can be as nice as any car. Their cabs are heated and cooled. They have comfortable seats for long drives. They may cost a lot of money!

In tractor pulls, the engine is changed to give it more power.

Tractor Pulling

Tractors are used for fun, too! Tractor pulling is a motorsport. Tractors pull superheavy objects a certain distance. Many people love to watch tractor pulls!

FAST FACT

The tractors in tractor pulls may look more like race cars than tractors!

Activity

Terrific Tractors!

Let's dig in!

Step 1: Make a 2-column chart on your poster board.

Step 2: The left column is titled: What Farmers Do.

Step 3: The right column is titled: How Tractors Help.

Step 4: Find out the many jobs farmers do on farms. Use library books or the internet, with the help of an adult. Fill in what you find in the left column of your chart.

Step 5: Do more research to find out how tractors help farmers do each job in the left column. Write in your findings in the right column.

Step 6: Give your chart a title.

LEARN MORE

Books

Dittmer, Lori. *Tractors*. Mankato, MN: Creative Education, 2018.

Oachs, Emily Rose. *Tractors*. Minneapolis, MN: Bellwether Media, 2017.

Weingarten, E. T. *Tractors*. New York, NY: Gareth Stevens Publishing, 2017.

Websites

Historical Timeline—Farm Machinery & Technology
www.agclassroom.org/gan/timeline/farm_tech.htm
Check out a timeline about farm inventions through the years.

John Deere for Kids
www.deere.com/en/connect-with-john-deere/john-deere-for-kids/
Watch videos of farm machines and learn about life on the farm.

INDEX

Published in 2020 by Enslow Publishing, LLC.
101 W. 23rd Street, Suite 240, New York, NY 10011

Library of Congress Cataloging-in-Publication Data

Names: Shea, Therese, author.
Title: Tractors / Therese M. Shea.
Description: New York : Enslow Publishing, 2020. | Series: Let's learn about farm machines | Includes bibliographical references and index. | Audience: Grades K-3.
Identifiers: LCCN 2019008570| ISBN 9781978513273 (library bound) | ISBN 9781978513259 (pbk.) | ISBN 9781978513266 (6 pack)
Subjects: LCSH: Tractors--Juvenile literature.
Classification: LCC TL233.15 .S543 2020 | DDC 631.3/72--dc23
LC record available at https://lccn.loc.gov/2019008570

Printed in the United States of America

Photos Credits: Cover, p. 1 smereka/Shutterstock.com; interior pages background landscape Jurgis Mankauskas/Shutterstock.com; p. 4 Mypurgatoryyears/iStock/Getty Images; pp. 5, 7, 9, 11, 13, 15, 17, 19, 22 (hay bale) photomaster/Shutterstock.com; p. 6 © iStockphoto.com/ChiccoDodiFC; p. 8 Kirn Vintage Stock/Corbis Historical/Getty Images; p. 10 hramovnick/Shutterstock.com (top); p. 10 chrism_nz/Shutterstock.com (bottom); p. 12 Bill & Brigitte Clough/Passage/Getty Images; p. 14 fotog/Getty Images; p. 16 Bill Bachmann/Alamy Stock Photo; p. 18 DeymosHR/Shutterstock.com; p. 20 picture alliance/Getty Images; p. 23 © iStockphoto.com/oticki; cover, p. 1 logo element (tractor) Krivosheev Vitaly/Shutterstock.com.